Susan Goodman • Sandy Hammer

ACTION BOOKS

LIFE SCIENCES

Published by
New Look Books
PO Box 864
Oxford
OX2 9YD

ISBN 1-901308-04-9

British Library Cataloguing in Publication Data.
A catalogue record for this book is available from the British Library.

Printed and bound in Great Britain.

Signs of life

Do you really know what is alive? Look at all the things below. (Ignore the multiplication sums for the moment.) Circle the ones you think are alive.

robot
9 x 9

tree
7 x 8

seaweed
4 x 9

raisin
3 x 7

seed
3 x 6

bread
3 x 7

mould
on bread
6 x 7

beefburger
9 x 3

fingernails
7 x 5

wool
7 x 7

television
9 x 7

Now check your answers by working out the multiplication sums. Only those with answers that are even numbers are alive.

moss
2 x 8

germs
7 x 6

In the following paragraph choose the correct word from the pairs of words in the brackets.

All living things need food to stay alive and grow. Animals eat other animals or plants. But plants can make (there, their) own food, using the process of photosynthesis. Plants use simple ingredients for this. They take water from the ground (through, threw) (there, their) roots, absorb carbon dioxide from the air, and use energy from the sun. This process takes place in green leaves.

eggs from
a shop
5 x 9

fossil
3 x 5

clouds
3 x 7

Food for thought

Proteins are part of every cell in your body. They form an important part of your daily diet. Look at the table below and work out how much protein Daniel, Katie and Emma eat on a typical day. They are all 10 years old and need about 30g of protein a day. Who ate enough protein?

Food	Amount	Protein (g)	Food	Amount	Protein (g)
Bread (two slices)	100g	9	Pizza	100g	15
Beefburger	100g	16	Cheddar cheese	100g	25
Fishfingers (four)	100g	16	Hazelnut	100g	16
Chips	100g	3	Ice-cream	100g	4
Baked beans	100g	5	Crisps	100g	7
Spaghetti	100g	2	Chocolate biscuits (five)	100g	3

Daniel
Breakfast: none

Lunch:
pizza, 100g

Dinner:
beefburger, 100g
baked beans, 50g
chips, 50g
ice-cream, 50g

Katie
Breakfast:
bread, 100g
cheese, 20g

Lunch:
spaghetti, 50g
cheese, 20g
ice-cream, 100g

Dinner:
4 fish fingers, 100g
baked beans, 50g
chips, 50g
ice-cream, 50g

Emma

Breakfast:
5 chocolate biscuits, 100g

Lunch:
crisps, 100g
5 chocolate biscuits, 100g

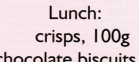

Dinner:
chips, 100g
ice-cream, 200g

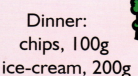

For a good diet you should also eat lots of fruit and vegetables.

Body-building

You need all sorts of different foods to have a balanced diet. These must include **proteins, carbohydrates, fats, fibre, mineral salts, vitamins and water.**

Proteins are body-building foods. Eating animals is a good source of protein, so are the seeds of some plants.

Carbohydrates give us energy. They are mainly made of starch and sugar.

Fats give us even more energy than carbohydrates. Fried foods contain a lot of fat.

Fibre is the part of your food which your body can't break down and absorb. It makes the muscles of your intestines work properly. It is found in fruit and vegetables.

Label these columns with one of the above food groups which most clearly describes the listed foods below.

fish	spaghetti	margarine	apples
beef	bread	butter	cabbage
cheese	potatoes	lard	bran
eggs	cake	oil	lettuce
beans	jam	chips	celery

Vitamins and **mineral salts** are essential in very small amounts to help us build and maintain strong, healthy bodies.

Loose links

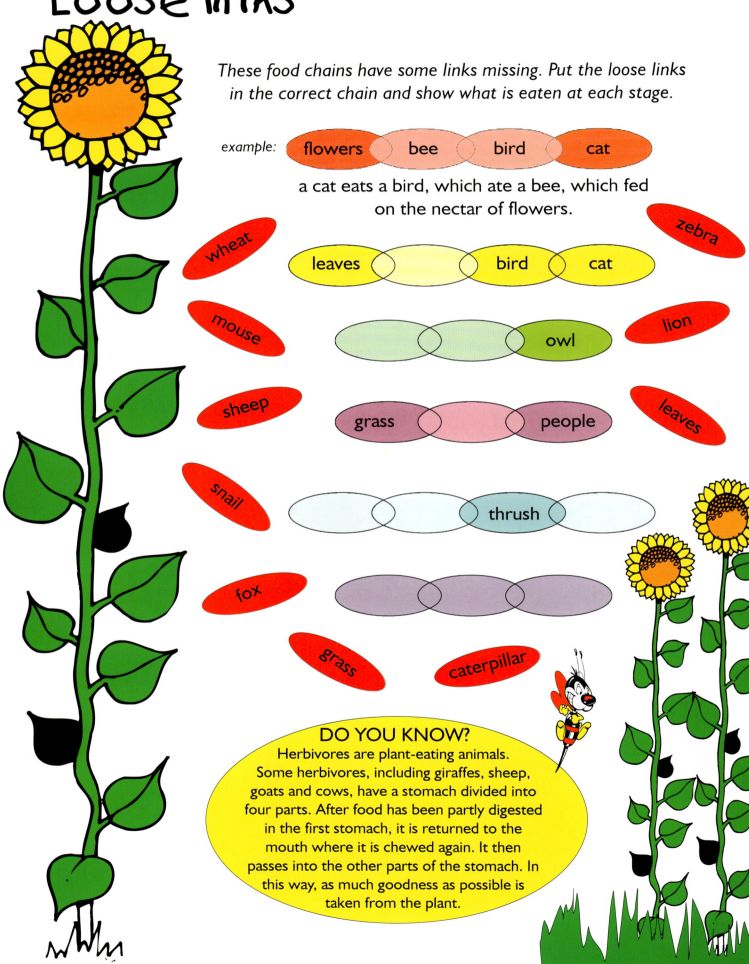

These food chains have some links missing. Put the loose links in the correct chain and show what is eaten at each stage.

example:

flowers — bee — bird — cat

a cat eats a bird, which ate a bee, which fed on the nectar of flowers.

wheat

zebra

leaves — ⬭ — bird — cat

mouse

lion

⬭ — ⬭ — owl

sheep

leaves

grass — ⬭ — people

snail

⬭ — thrush — ⬭

fox

⬭ — ⬭ — ⬭

grass

caterpillar

DO YOU KNOW?
Herbivores are plant-eating animals. Some herbivores, including giraffes, sheep, goats and cows, have a stomach divided into four parts. After food has been partly digested in the first stomach, it is returned to the mouth where it is chewed again. It then passes into the other parts of the stomach. In this way, as much goodness as possible is taken from the plant.

Hide and seek

Find the mystery numbers.

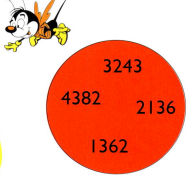

1. It is even.
   The digits add up to 12.
   The thousands digit is odd.

3243
4382   2136
1362

2. It is between 160 and 285.
   It is odd.
   The digits add up to an odd number.
   It can be divided by 3.

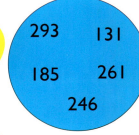

293   131
185   261
246

3. It is even.
   It can be divided by 8.
   The hundreds digit and the units digit
   are the same.

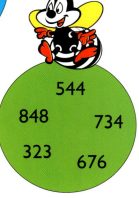

544
848   734
323   676

Now find the mystery animal corresponding to each mystery number.

1362
woodlouse

2136
bee

293
mouse

676
flower

261
worm

848
slug

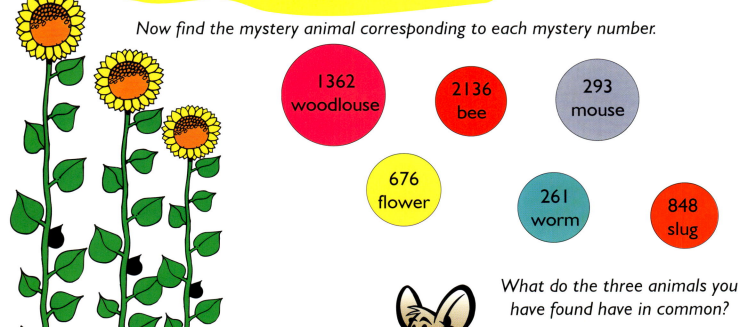

*What do the three animals you
have found have in common?*

Inside crossword

Across

1. It carries oxygen to every part of you.
6. Stores some glucose sugar and prepares food for use in other parts of the body.
7. A long tube which carries food from your stomach.
9. It carries blood away from the heart.
10. They make you move.

Down

2. Air enters these.
3. They help clean your blood.
4. A blood vessel which carries blood towards the heart.
5. It pumps blood.
8. Your food stays here for about 3 hours after you swallow it.

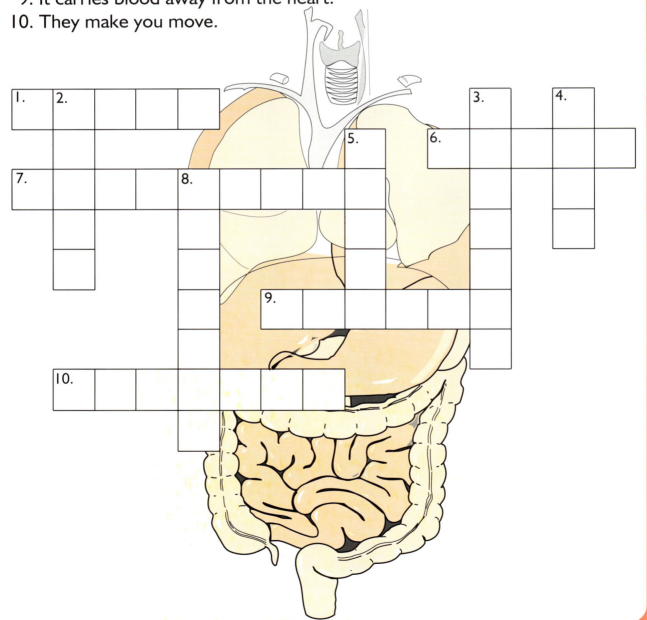

Teething problems

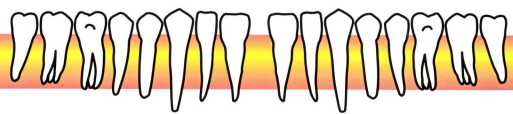

Read this story about Candy and her teeth. Then answer the sums below.

When Candy was born she was toothless, like most babies. At a year old she had four front teeth, two at the top and two at the bottom. These sharp *incisors* were great for biting apples, cheese, and biscuits. And when she clamped her teeth on her brother's arm, she drew blood. When Candy was two years old she had a full set of 20 *milk teeth*. At the front, eight *incisors* and also four pointed *canine* teeth; at the back, eight *premolars* with large, uneven top surfaces, ideal for chewing and grinding. She chomped toast at breakfast, sausages at lunch, and pizza for dinner. She also exercised her jaws chewing on socks, shoes and sweets - especially sweets. There was only one thing she would not allow into her mouth - a toothbrush! By the age of five, four teeth were decayed and had been drilled and filled by the dentist.

1. When Candy was one year old, what percentage of her teeth were incisors?

2. At the age of two, what fraction of her teeth did she use for chewing?

3. At five years old, what fraction of her milk teeth had fillings in them?

4. Put these fractions in increasing order, with the smallest first:

$$\frac{1}{20} \qquad \frac{1}{8} \qquad \frac{1}{4} \qquad \frac{1}{10}$$

5. Put these fractions in decreasing order, with the largest first:

$$\frac{3}{5} \qquad \frac{3}{4} \qquad \frac{3}{10} \qquad \frac{7}{20}$$

Spineless sums

All the animals in the world are divided by scientists into two main groups :
1. vertebrates (meaning animals with backbones), including humans, horses, birds, snakes, and elephants.
2. invertebrates (meaning animals without backbones), including insects, shellfish, octopus, and spiders.

In the puzzle below, begin at the letter (S) *and solve the multiplication sums. Travel to a letter which gives a correct answer. Then continue from that letter and keep going until you have the name of an invertebrate. There are five different invertebrates all beginning with* (S) .

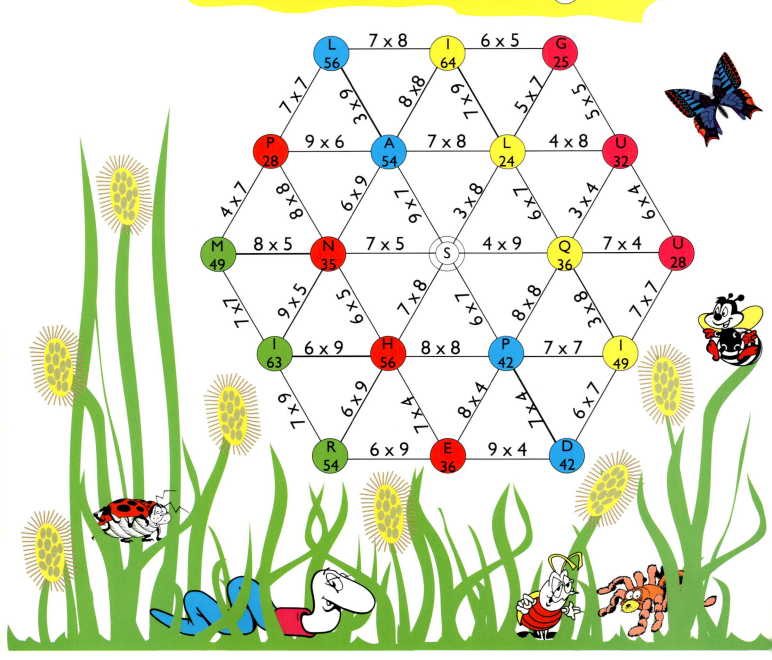

Garden pairs

Most of the animals you find in the garden, or park, are invertebrates (with no backbone).
Below you can see the names of invertebrates split into two parts.
Join the parts together. And make a list of the animals you find.

pillar

sn

wood

ug

der

louse

cater

wo

spi

beet

ail

mo

pede

but

rm

sp

dragon

th

le

fly

centi

sl

terfly

wa

Snake bites

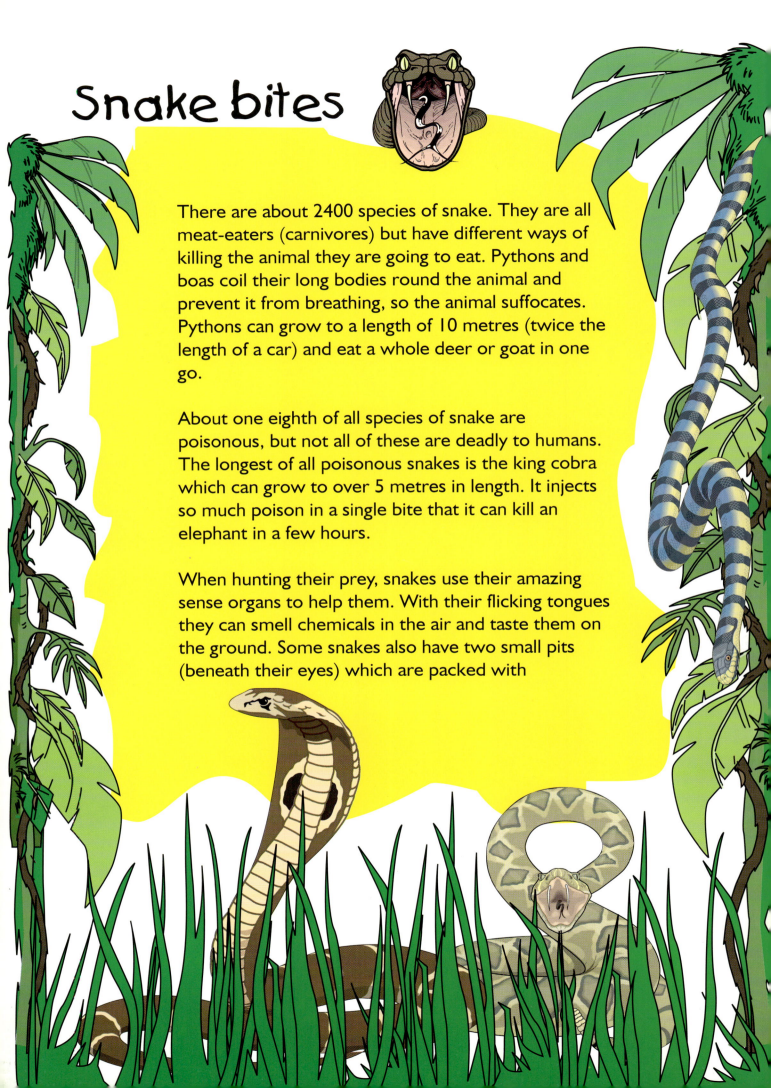

There are about 2400 species of snake. They are all meat-eaters (carnivores) but have different ways of killing the animal they are going to eat. Pythons and boas coil their long bodies round the animal and prevent it from breathing, so the animal suffocates. Pythons can grow to a length of 10 metres (twice the length of a car) and eat a whole deer or goat in one go.

About one eighth of all species of snake are poisonous, but not all of these are deadly to humans. The longest of all poisonous snakes is the king cobra which can grow to over 5 metres in length. It injects so much poison in a single bite that it can kill an elephant in a few hours.

When hunting their prey, snakes use their amazing sense organs to help them. With their flicking tongues they can smell chemicals in the air and taste them on the ground. Some snakes also have two small pits (beneath their eyes) which are packed with

heat-sensitive nerve cells. The rattlesnake, for example, can detect a temperature rise of only a few hundredths of a degree Celsius. In total darkness it can accurately locate a small animal a metre away. The rattlesnake's head then shoots forward at a speed of 3 metres per second and sinks its poisonous fangs into the helpless animal.

From what you have just read about snakes, decide if the statements below are true or false. Tick the boxes.

	True	False
1. There are more than 800 species of poisonous snake.	☐	☐
2. A snake's heat-sensitive pits can detect a temperature rise of 0.0001°C.	☐	☐
3. A fully-grown king cobra is less than half the size of the largest pythons.	☐	☐
4. The rattlesnake can shoot its head forward at a speed equal to 180 metres per minute.	☐	☐
5. The number of snake species is equal to about 2.4 x 1000.	☐	☐

Rabbiting on......

Rabbits belong to the group of animals called 'mammals'. All mammals are warm blooded, often with fur or hair to keep them warm. In most mammals the babies grow inside the mother's body. When born, all baby mammals feed on milk produced by their mothers.

Rabbits also belong to the group called 'rodents'. They all have special front teeth for gnawing food. Their teeth are worn down by this process, but they carry on growing right through the animal's life.

Look at the group of animals below. Put each in its right box in the diagram.

pigeon   cat   hedgehog   whale

goldfish   adder   rabbit   human

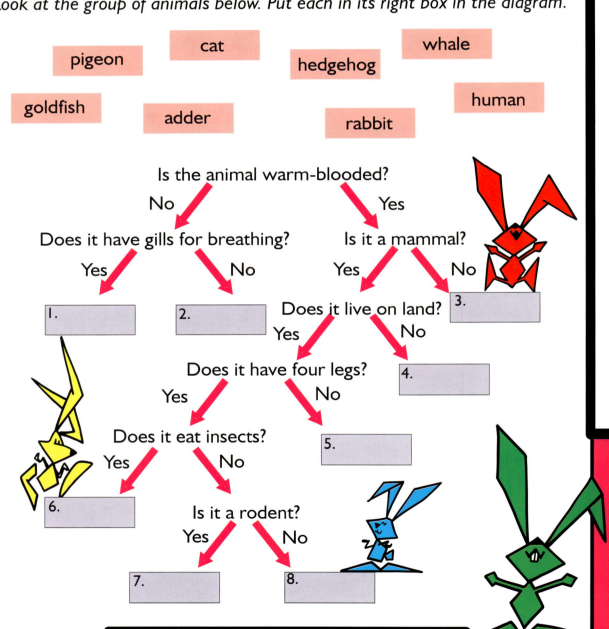

Is the animal warm-blooded?

No → Does it have gills for breathing?

Yes → Is it a mammal?

Does it have gills for breathing?
Yes → 1. ☐
No → 2. ☐

Is it a mammal?
Yes → Does it live on land?
No → 3. ☐

Does it live on land?
Yes → Does it have four legs?
No → 4. ☐

Does it have four legs?
Yes → Does it eat insects?
No → 5. ☐

Does it eat insects?
Yes → 6. ☐
No → Is it a rodent?

Is it a rodent?
Yes → 7. ☐
No → 8. ☐

and on.....

You can see from the chart below that there are many breeds of pet rabbit, and that they range widely in size.

Change the weights listed here from kilograms (kg) to grams (g).

Breed	Usual colour	Weight (kg)	Weight (g)
English Lop	various	9	
Flemish Giant	steel-grey	5	
English Satin	various	3	
Angora	white	2¾	
Dutch	black and white	2¼	
Dwarf Lop	various	2	
Netherland Dwarf	various	1	

Supposing you weigh 36kg. How many times heavier are you than these breeds of rabbit?

a) English Lop
b) English Satin
c) Dutch
d) Dwarf Lop
e) Netherland Dwarf

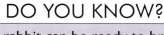

DO YOU KNOW?

A female rabbit can be ready to breed at six months old. After mating, the young are born about a month (31 days) later. She gives birth to about six young (kittens). Two months later the young rabbits are no longer feeding on her milk. The mother rabbit might mate again!
How many rabbits could she give birth to in a year?

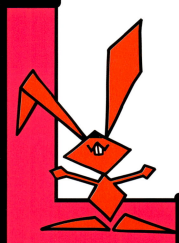

Eye can see

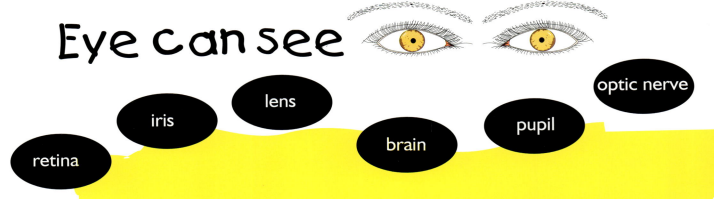

retina iris lens brain pupil optic nerve

The eyeball is slightly smaller than a golf ball and is hollow inside. At the front of the eye is a coloured disc called the _ _ _ _. Light enters the eye through the _ _ _ _ _, the small black hole in the centre of the iris. The light is focussed by the _ _ _ _ of the eye and forms a picture on the _ _ _ _ _ _ at the back of the eye. Here, light-sensitive cells send messages as tiny electrical impulses to the _ _ _ _ _ along the _ _ _ _ _ _ _ _ _ _.

Now use the above list of words to label the boxes in this diagram of the eye.

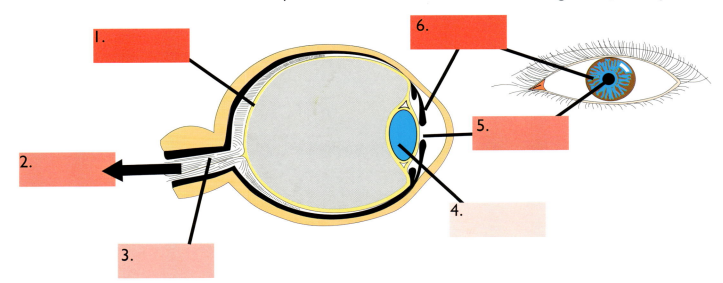

1.

6.

2.

5.

4.

3.

Blinking problem
Blinking keeps your eyes clean and moist. Normally you blink every six seconds and your eyes stay closed for one sixth of a second. Work out approximately how long your eyes stay closed in a minute, then in an hour. Assume you are awake 15 hours a day, how long will your blinking eyes be closed? How long will they be closed during a year? Work it out approximately.

Noisy numbers

Noise is measured in decibels (db). The bar graph shows different levels of noise. Each bubble on the right describes a different noise. Match these noises with the correct decibel level shown on the bar graph.

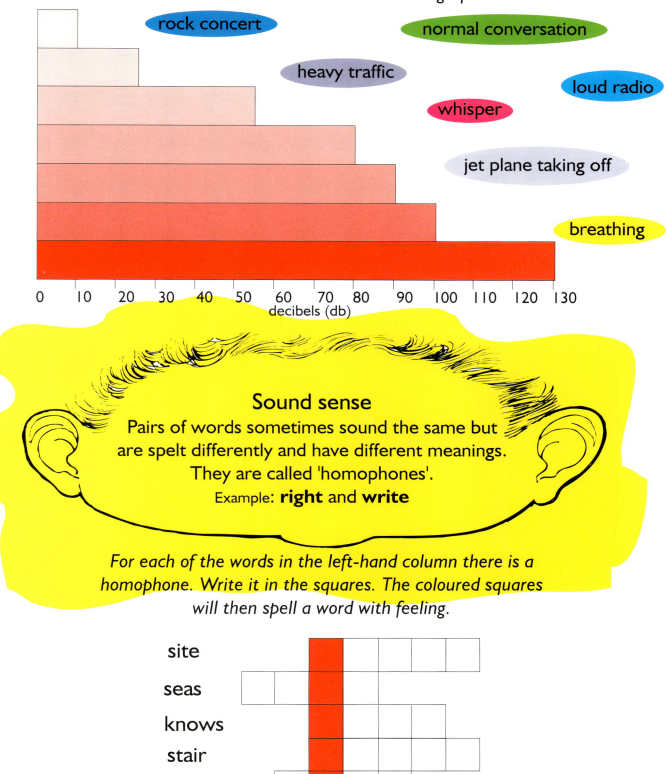

rock concert

normal conversation

heavy traffic

loud radio

whisper

jet plane taking off

breathing

decibels (db)

0 10 20 30 40 50 60 70 80 90 100 110 120 130

Sound sense
Pairs of words sometimes sound the same but are spelt differently and have different meanings. They are called 'homophones'.
Example: **right** and **write**

For each of the words in the left-hand column there is a homophone. Write it in the squares. The coloured squares will then spell a word with feeling.

site

seas

knows

stair

here

Plant puzzle

Rearrange the letters to spell a part of the plant below and so label the picture.

1. lptea

2. agtsmi

3. mntsae

4. yrvao

5. sleap

6. fale

7. ostor

8. smte

See how many words you can make from the word

POLLINATION

10: average
15: very good
20: excellent

DO YOU KNOW?

Roots take up water and minerals from the soil. They also stop a plant falling over. There are two main types of root: fibrous roots and tap roots. Fibrous roots grow out a long way, like those in the picture. Tap roots are thick, swollen roots which store food, like carrots or parsnips.

Flower power

Fill in the missing words in the yellow passage below using the green grid references.

	A	B	C	D
3	flies	stigma	brushes	scented
2	feeds	travels	settles	grow
1	sticky	coloured	lands	attract

Petals are often brightly (B,1) so that they (D,1) insects to the flower. Many flowers are also strongly (D,3) to bring in insect visitors. An insect (C,2) on a flower and (A,2) on the sweet nectar at the base of the petals. While feeding, the insect accidentally (C,3) past the stamens. A fine yellow dust, called 'pollen', comes off the stamens and onto the insect. When the insect (A,3) and (C,1) on another flower of the same kind of plant, some pollen (C,2) on the (A,1) stigma. The pollen (B,2) down the tube of the (B,3) into the ovary and a seed will then begin to (D,2). This is called 'pollination'.

DO YOU KNOW?
Some garden flowers, such as daffodils, tulips, hyacinths, and snowdrops, grow from bulbs. Onions are bulbs, and if you plant one in the ground it will produce leaves and flowers. A bulb is really a large store of food from which the plant grows. If you cut an onion in half you can see that the food is stored in layers.

Bodyparts wordsearch

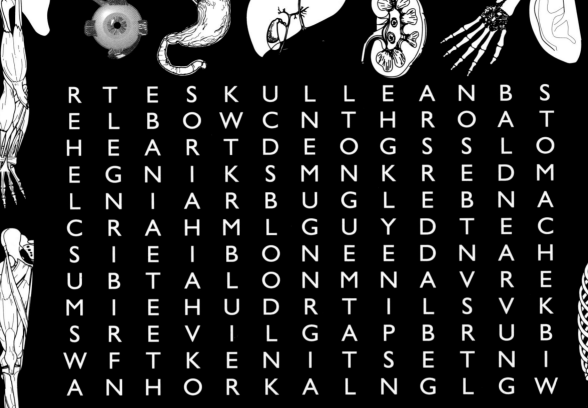

```
R  T  E  S  K  U  L  L  E  A  N  B  S
E  L  B  O  W  C  N  T  H  R  O  A  T
H  E  A  R  T  D  E  O  G  S  R  L  O
E  G  N  I  K  S  M  N  K  R  E  D  M
L  N  I  A  R  B  U  G  L  E  B  N  A
C  R  A  H  M  L  G  U  Y  D  T  E  C
S  I  E  I  B  O  N  E  E  D  N  A  H
U  B  T  A  L  O  N  M  E  A  R  R  E
M  I  E  H  U  D  R  T  I  L  S  V  K
S  R  E  V  I  L  G  A  P  B  R  U  B
W  F  T  K  E  N  I  T  S  E  T  N  I
A  N  H  O  R  K  A  L  N  G  L  G  W
```

Go forwards, backwards, up, down, and diagonally.
Find all the words listed below. Colour the letters as you find the words

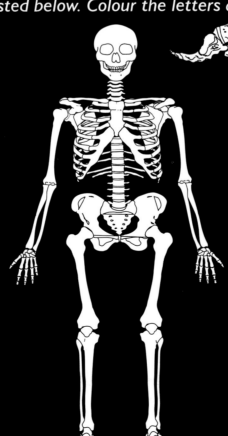

HEART
HAIR
BRAIN
TONGUE
NAIL
BLOOD
LUNG
TEETH
SKULL
SPINE
BLADDER
ELBOW
TOE
GUM
SKIN

MUSCLE
NERVE
NOSE
INTESTINE
LEG
HAND
RIB
NECK
EYE
EAR
THROAT
STOMACH
KIDNEY
LIVER
BONE

Bone breaker

In the sentences below, the names of bones and joints are missing. Each bone fragment contains one of these words with the letters mixed up.

1. The _____ protects your brain.

2. Two hip bones make up the _____

3. The _____ is the largest bone in the body.

4. Heart and lungs are protected by the _____

5. At the _____ the foot is joined to the leg.

6. The _____ is made of lots of small bones called 'vertebrae'.

7. The ulna and radius join the hand bones at the _____

8. The shin bone is called the _____

9. The _____ is the joint where the arm bones meet.

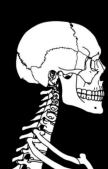

ANSWERS

Signs of life
Living things are: seed, 18; germs, 42; tree, 56; mould, 42; seaweed, 36; moss, 16.
their, through, their.

Body-building
Going from left to right: proteins, carbohydrates, fats, fibre.

Food for thought
Daniel: 37g protein; Katie: 46g protein; Emma: 24g protein.
Daniel and Katie ate sufficient protein.

Loose links
leaves, caterpillar or snail, bird, cat; wheat, mouse, owl; grass, cow, people; leaves, caterpillar or snail, thrush, fox; grass, zebra, lion.

Hide and seek
1362, woodlouse; 261, worm; 848, slug.
They all live in damp, dark places. If you read the page 'Spineless sums' in this book, you will discover they are all **invertebrates.**

Inside crossword
Across: 1. blood, 6. liver, 7. intestine, 9. artery, 10. muscles
Down: 2. lungs, 3. kidneys, 4. vein, 5. heart, 8. stomach

Teething problems
1. 100%

2. $\frac{8}{20}$ or $\frac{2}{5}$

3. $\frac{4}{20}$ or $\frac{1}{5}$

4. $\frac{1}{20}$ $\frac{1}{10}$ $\frac{1}{8}$ $\frac{1}{4}$

5. $\frac{3}{4}$ $\frac{3}{5}$ $\frac{7}{20}$ $\frac{3}{10}$

Spineless sums
SLUG, SPIDER, SHRIMP, SQUID, SNAIL

ANSWERS

Garden pairs
snail, butterfly, caterpillar, centipede, slug, spider, woodlouse, worm, beetle, dragonfly, moth, wasp.

Snake bites
False, false, false, true, true.

Rabbiting on..
1. goldfish, 2. adder, 3. pigeon, 4. whale, 5. human, 6. hedgehog, 7. rabbit, 8. cat.

and on......
9000g, 5000g, 3000g, 2750g, 2250g, 2000g, 1000g
a) 4,   b) 12,   c) 16,   d) 18,   e) 36.
A fully-grown female rabbit could give birth to 24 kittens a year.

Eye can see
Iris, pupil, lens, retina, brain, optic nerve.
1. retina, 2. brain, 3. optic nerve, 4. lens, 5. pupil, 6. iris.
Eyes blink closed about 180 hours in a year. (see CLUES page.)

Noisy numbers
breathing, 10db; whisper, 25db; conversation, 55db;
heavy traffic, 80db; loud radio, 90db; rock concert, 100db;
jet plane taking off, 130db.
Sight, sees, nose, stare, hear. Sense.

Flower power
coloured, attract, scented, settles, feeds, brushes, flies, lands, sticky, travels, stigma, grow.

Plant puzzle
1. petal, 2. stigma, 3. stamen, 4. ovary, 5. sepal, 6. leaf, 7. roots, 8. stem.

Bonebreaker
1. skull, 2. pelvis, 3. femur, 4. ribs, 5. ankle, 6. spine, 7. wrist, 8. tibia, 9. elbow.

CLUES

Signs of life

Seeds don't seem to be alive, but add water and they grow. Seeds are in a sort of sleeping state.

Food for thought

Check the amount of each food eaten and then work out how much protein has been eaten. For example: 50g chips has 1½g of protein.

Loose links

Work out the ones you know, and cross out the loose links as you use them, so that you can see what is left.
Example: flowers, bee, bird, cat.

Hide and seek

Cross out the numbers that can't be the mystery number.

Inside crossword

The answer to 7. Across is INTESTINE, 9. Across is ARTERY.

Teething problems

1. All her teeth were incisors. Write this as a percentage.
2. 8 out of 20 were used for chewing. Write as a fraction.
3. 4 out of 20 were filled. Write as a fraction.
4. The larger the number on the bottom, the smaller the fraction.
5. Change all the fractions so that they have 20 on the bottom.

Always multiply the top and bottom of each fraction by the same number. For example:

$$\frac{1}{10} = \frac{2}{20}, \quad \frac{3}{10} = \frac{6}{20}, \quad \frac{1}{4} = \frac{5}{20}$$

Garden pairs

There are 14 different animals. Join up the most obvious pairs, then see what is left.

Snake bites

1. One eighth of all snakes are poisonous. Find one eighth of 2400.
2. 0.0001 is much less than a hundredth. A hundredth is 0.01.
   0.0001 is a ten thousandth.
3. The largest python is 10 metres long. Half of a python's length is 5 metres.
4. Multiply by 60 to change metres per second to metres per minute.
5. 2.4×10=24. Now try 2.4×100, then 2.4×1000.

Rabbiting on...and on...

1kg=1000g, ½kg=500g, ¼kg=250g
When working out how many times heavier 36kg is than 9kg, divide 36 by 9. In c) notice that 4×2¼=9
A female rabbit can give birth to 6 young every 3 months.

Eye can see

In six seconds eyes blink closed for 1/6 sec. Now work out for a minute, an hour, 15 hours. Then assume 25 minutes is about half an hour. You may use a calculator.

Noisy numbers

All the homophones are to do with your senses.

Bonebreaker

Here are the words: skull, spine, ribs, ankle, tibia, elbow, femur, wrist, pelvis. Now put them in the correct sentences.